The Mandala of the Five Buddhas

Vessantara

The Mandala of
the Five Buddhas

WINDHORSE PUBLICATIONS

Published by Windhorse Publications
11 Park Road, Birmingham, B13 8AB

Based on Part Two of *Meeting the Buddhas*,
Windhorse Publications, 1993

Printed by Interprint Ltd
Marsa, Malta
Cover design: Dhammarati

British Library Cataloguing in Publication Data:
A catalogue record for this book is available from the British Library.
ISBN 1 899579 16 8

Since this work is intended for a general readership, Pali and Sanskrit
words have been transliterated without the diacritical marks which
would have been appropriate in a work of a more scholarly nature.

CONTENTS

Preface 1

1 The Origin of the Five Buddhas 5

2 Akshobhya: The Imperturbable 16

3 Ratnasambhava: The Jewel-Born 25

4 Amitabha: Infinite Light 37

5 Amoghasiddhi: Unobstructed Success 46

6 Vairochana: The Illuminator 58

Conclusion 69

Illustration Credits 77

Index 79

About the Author

Vessantara is a senior member of the Western Buddhist Order. Born Tony McMahon in London in 1950, he gained an M.A. in English at Cambridge University. Interested in Buddhism since his teens, he first had direct contact with Buddhists in 1971. In 1974 he became a member of the Western Buddhist Order and was given the name Vessantara, which means 'universe within'. In 1975 he gave up a career in social work to become chairman of the Brighton Buddhist Centre. Since then he has divided his time between meditating, studying, and aiding the development of several Buddhist centres, including retreat centres in England, Wales, and Spain.

For six years he was secretary to Sangharakshita, the founder of the Western Buddhist Order, and for seven years he led three-month courses for people entering the Order, including helping them prepare to take up the visualization of many of the figures described in this book.

He is much in demand as a Buddhist teacher, giving talks and leading retreats and workshops in Europe and Australasia. He is now based in Birmingham, where he works as one of a group of Order members to whom Sangharakshita has passed on his responsibilities.

PREFACE

TEN YEARS AGO I was living in a mountain valley in
south-east Spain, at a Buddhist retreat centre known as
Guhyaloka, 'the Secret Realm'. Whilst the community
who lived there didn't necessarily have any secrets, we
were certainly hard to find, and very isolated from the
world. We had no TV, radio, or telephone. Picking up
mail involved a half-hour of lurching and bumping to
the nearest village in our aged Land-Rover. After heavy
rain the trip was perilous, as we launched off down the
mud-covered track below the valley in a controlled slide,
struggling not to slither off the unguarded left edge,
with the dubious consolation of knowing that if we did
there would be time to recite plenty of mantras before
we hit the bottom.

We lived very close to nature. There were eagles and
nightingales, adders and orchids, wild boar and all kinds
of butterflies. At times nature came a little too close for
comfort, as when electrical storms burst over the valley,

lightning seared the holm oaks, and the thunder rolled along the limestone cliffs, playing them like ancient bass drums.

I lived in a small plaster hut and spent much of my time writing a book. Into it I was trying to distil the essence of my understanding of Buddhist symbols, and in particular of the wondrous figures which have come down to us within the Indo-Tibetan tradition of Buddhism. Meditations on these symbolic figures, expressing different facets of the experience of Enlightenment, are some of the most potent tools for self-transformation that we have available to us as human beings. Through contemplating them we can catalyse profound changes in our minds, imbuing our monochrome everyday experience with the rich colours cast by the inner sun in the depths of our being.

So I sat in the Secret Realm, striving to evoke those magical figures, to immerse myself in their world, and to write about them not as symbols but as living experiences. When the writing went badly I would go out and pace up and down under the vast Spanish sky, repeating the mantra, the sound symbol, of the figure about which I was writing. At times when it went well I felt a happiness which was too simple to put into words.

Eventually the job was done, and the result was called *Meeting the Buddhas*. That book looked at all the most common figures found in the Indo-Tibetan tradition: Buddhas, Bodhisattvas, and tantric deities. It has proved very popular, but it is a five-course meal of a book, running to 350 pages. So Windhorse Publications suggested using material from it to produce a much shorter introduction to a central set of figures – the Five Buddhas – which would be valuable in its own right and would serve as an entrée to the much more substantial fare in *Meeting the Buddhas*. All the material here, apart from the Conclusion, has been extracted from that book. If you appreciate it, I hope you will be inspired to read the fuller treatment of the Five Buddhas and the other figures in that larger work.

This book is the first of a planned series, introducing some of the central symbols of the Buddhist tradition. Symbols are very important for Buddhism, as it aims to bring about a radical transformation of all aspects of ourselves – including both our heads and our hearts. Thus it communicates using both rational discussion and a highly-developed second language: a cornucopia of symbol, myth, and poetry. The symbols of this second language emerged out of profound states of consciousness, in the meditations, dreams, and inspirations of people who had fathomed the mysteries of reality. Thus Buddhist symbols have the power to awaken us to new potentials of our minds, and to speak to levels of our being on which rational argument is dumb.

In learning about Buddhist symbols, the mandala of the Five Buddhas is a good place to start. An understanding of it is crucial in order to place all the other symbolic figures in context. It furnishes the ground-plan for the whole symbolic edifice of Tibetan Buddhism, as well as for Shingon, the tantric Buddhism of Japan. It can also provide a ground-plan for our lives, giving us a set of symbols to contemplate which will draw our lives into harmony and put us in contact with that inner sun.

We live in a world in which the power of symbols is no longer much appreciated – except by advertisers and politicians, who attempt to colonize images of power and apply them to trivial and frequently manipulative ends, so that tigers end up scratching a living selling petrol. The Buddhist tradition, by contrast, employs the power of symbols to communicate aspects of Enlightenment. The contemplation of Buddhism's central symbols, such as the Five Buddhas, can lead us beyond trivia and manipulation, beyond all egotistical concerns, into a world of peace and beauty, love and joy, in which we experience the majesty of the mind set free.

I very much appreciate the efforts of all those connected with Windhorse Publications who have helped bring this project to fruition. I would particularly like to thank Virachitta, who came up with the original idea, and produced an edited version of a chapter of *Meeting the Buddhas* to show how it could work.

Vessantara
Birmingham
January 1999

1

THE ORIGIN OF THE FIVE BUDDHAS

HISTORICALLY there was one Buddha, Shakyamuni, who lived in Northern India two and a half thousand years ago and who taught the path to Enlightenment. But if you are familiar with Buddhist art or have visited Buddhist centres or temples, you are likely to have seen many different Buddhas depicted. Where did these other figures appear from?

Naturally, Shakyamuni, in whom Enlightenment first flowered in this historical age, has always been honoured and remembered by his followers. The story of his struggle and spiritual victory has been dwelt on by generations of Buddhists. People meditating deeply on his life have discovered layers of meaning to his story, and many facets to Enlightenment. We know that after the Buddha's passing away many of his disciples worked at ways of achieving visions of him. 'Recollection of the Buddha' seems to have been an important meditation practice in early Buddhism, bringing forth

devotion and emotional richness through contemplation of the qualities of an Enlightened being. As experienced meditators focused on particular qualities of
Shakyamuni other, archetypal, figures arose from the
depths of their minds.

Archetypes can be understood as deep patterns within
our mind. We may become aware of them when we have
experiences which feel charged with symbolic significance. It is as if archetypal material taps into experiences
which are not personal to us, but go far back into the past
and are common to all human beings. For example, in
myths and dreams fundamental aspects of life such as
the sun, moon, stars, mother, and father appear as powerful symbols. There is something about such experiences that seems to go beyond both our rational mind
and our individual circumstances. They are often very
moving, having a timeless quality and a heightened
sense of meaning. Dwelling on something that acts as an
archetypal symbol for us can produce deep and positive
changes within our minds.

Over the centuries, out of deep meditation on the
Enlightened qualities which Shakyamuni embodied,
thousands of these archetypal figures appeared within
the Buddhist tradition. Each is rich in symbolic meaning.
They express, through colour and form, an experience
that goes far beyond the range of normal human experience. They communicate the extraordinary experience
of Enlightenment and so could be called transcendental
archetypes. There are a great number of these figures
because Enlightenment is like a jewel that can be looked

at from different points of view. One is looking at the same jewel, and yet it has different facets, such as wisdom, compassion, peace, love, freedom, energy. Each of these figures brings us into contact with particular facets of Enlightenment.

Tracing back this development, it appears that, to begin with, two new Buddhas appeared (and here we are speaking the language of myth, not describing a historical process). These expressed the two great aspects of Enlightenment – Wisdom and Compassion. As people dwelt on those qualities as embodied in Shakyamuni, so they took on a life of their own, and became two new archetypal Buddhas – figures rich in symbolic meaning. Their forms grew out of his central figure, to flank him. In time, two more Buddhas appeared, whom we might call the Buddha of Generosity, or of Beauty, and the Buddha of Action. These took up their posts at the other two cardinal points around the central Buddha. The central figure of Shakyamuni, too, cast off the rags and wrinkles of the historical Buddha and appeared in a new and dazzling form. It is these five archetypal Buddhas whom we shall be meeting in this book.

When we meet with one or other of the Buddhist archetypal figures – whether in a painting or in meditation – we are brought face to face with a being who embodies Enlightenment, whose smile warms us with compassion, and whose eyes shine with the understanding of the nature of Reality – of things as they really are. An encounter with such a figure is likely to move us far more deeply than a list of the qualities of someone who is Enlightened. They do not just embody qualities such as wisdom and compassion, they can communicate a message to us about our potential as human beings. Thus each of the archetypal Buddhas is a vision of what we can become.

The four Buddhas seated at the cardinal points and the fifth central figure collectively form a mandala pattern. The word mandala can just mean circle. But in this case it means a visual symbol used in meditation, in which a number of elements are arranged in a satisfying pattern around a central focus. This mandala arrangement has a particular power to it. Through meditation it can become for us a symbol of the integration of different levels and aspects of our being.

The mandala is a universal symbol. Mandala designs are found in sacred circles in magical and religious traditions. For instance, there are fine examples in the 'sand paintings' of the Navaho Indians. Mandalas form an important aspect of both Hindu and Buddhist art and meditative practice.

More surprisingly, C.G. Jung found mandalas when working with his patients. Jung's goal was to catalyse the process of what he called 'individuation' – to make conscious different aspects of the psyche and bring them into harmony. Patients in whom this process was nearing completion frequently dreamt of mandalas. These were usually circular patterns within which four aspects were arranged around a central point. The people who produced them usually knew nothing about Buddhism or Navaho Indians, they just found the mandalas within their own minds. Drawing or painting mandalas gave them a feeling of wholeness. They could not say why, but there was something deeply satisfying about those particular patterns.

We have described a mandala as a symbol of integration of different levels or aspects of our being. However, this integration can be taken to different depths. Buddhism aims at a level of development far beyond that of the 'individuation' of Jung. It is a path to the very highest goal which a human being can attain. For a mandala to promote this deepest possible integration and harmonization of all aspects of our being, it needs to centre upon some aspect of Enlightenment, such as perfect wisdom or limitless compassion, as represented by Shakyamuni or one of the figures we shall meet in this book.

Meditating on a Buddhist mandala can enable us to go beyond all limited, unsatisfactory ways of being and to unfold the full potential of our consciousness. In the process, it can make us more aware of undeveloped aspects of ourselves. In spiritual practice there is a tendency to keep on developing one's strengths without addressing one's weaker faculties. You can keep on 'putting your best foot forward' on a spiritual level until it is so far in front of the other that you are in danger of falling over! In an ideal mandala all spiritual qualities will be represented in a harmonious pattern. This encourages you to develop all those qualities in a balanced way. It is a basic principle of Buddhism that whatever you set your heart and mind upon, that you become. So if you repeatedly meditate on an ideal mandala, your mind increasingly takes on that harmonious pattern, and eventually becomes in accord with reality itself.

Meditating on mandalas is an important practice in one particular form of Buddhism – called Tantra – which makes great use of visualization, symbolic ritual, and meditations that work with psychophysical energies. The Buddhist texts that describe these practices are also called Tantras, and they describe many thousands of mandalas. Some centre upon just one figure; others include hundreds. For the purposes of this book, it will be enough to look at some features that are common to many mandalas, and then examine the world of the five Buddhas in detail.

When you see pictures of Buddhist mandalas, you may have the impression that they are two-dimensional. However, what is shown in murals and hangings is just a diagram, a ground-plan. Mandalas are really three-dimensional. They represent the residence of the Buddha or other figure whose mandala it is. It is rather like seeing a map of a stately home, together with its grounds and perimeter wall. However, the mandala is not open to spiritual tourists; to enter the 'divine mansion' at its centre you have to be planning to make it your home. In fact you have to aspire to become one with the Enlightened consciousness of the figure at the centre. So let us explore the mandala a little, starting from the outside and working inwards.

The perimeter wall of a mandala actually consists of a number of concentric circles. The outermost is usually a great ring of flames. This forms a barrier that prevents anything negative from entering. One can pass through it only if one is prepared to be transformed in the process. In many religious traditions flames represent transformation from a grosser to a subtler mode of being.

Fire changes the nature of things, so for Buddhism it is a symbol of wisdom. Fire reveals to us that there is no inner essence to things, nothing that remains the same. This lack of any permanent, unchanging essence Buddhism sees as the ultimate nature of all existence and calls Emptiness or shunyata. Buddhism talks especially of the 'flames of shunyata' – the wisdom of Emptiness. If you take ice and heat it, it will all become water; if you carry on heating the water, it will become steam. The fire demonstrates that there is just a process of transformation – water arising in dependence upon heating ice, steam arising in dependence upon heating water. Nothing is fixed or immutable.

So the ring of flames symbolizes the transforming power of wisdom. It also shows us that entering the mandala involves being prepared to give ourselves up to a process of total transformation, after which nothing will remain of our 'old self'. To show that these are wisdom-fires, they are usually represented in five colours – the colours associated with the Wisdoms of the five Buddhas whom we shall soon meet.

If we pass through the ring of flames, we come to another protective barrier: a great wall surmounted by a tent-like structure, all made of stylized diamond thunderbolts, or vajras. The vajra is one of the most important of all Buddhist symbols. It has both the nature of a diamond – which can cut anything but cannot itself be cut – and the irresistible power of a thunderbolt. It thus represents a fusion of what is most dense and unbreachable with energy in its most ungraspable form. The vajra has the dynamic effect of a thunderbolt on other things, but cannot itself be affected. In Buddhism it becomes a symbol for Reality itself. More generally, it is a symbol for energy which cannot be stopped. Hence it represents the unshakeable determination and commitment that is needed to arrive at the centre of the mandala.

A vajra

In many mandalas there is one more protective circle to pass through. This gentlest circle is a ring of lotuses. These symbolize purity and renunciation. The lotus renounces first the mud in which it was born and then the water in which it has grown, to open its petals to the sunlight – petals that are unstained by its earthy birth. So the lotus represents purity, and rebirth on a higher level. In all Buddhist art and practice the lotus is a symbol of the transcendental – of what has gone beyond the mud of the world, has risen above even the gentle waters of mundane positive mental states, and now basks in the sunlight of Reality.

Within the ring of lotuses stands the divine mansion itself. This is usually four-sided, with a gate at each of the cardinal points. It is beautiful, adorned with exquisite hangings and precious things. Often its colour is variegated to fit in with the symbolism of the mandala as a whole.

It is usual to enter a mandala from the east – which is the direction in which the sun rises to light the world anew. For this reason, in pictures of mandalas, the bottom is always the eastern direction (and not the south, as on most maps).

Mandalas, like houses, vary in their complexity. They may have just one level, or as many as five. Entering the divine mansion we may find many occupants or just one. Every aspect of the mandala – the protective circles, the residence and its inhabitants, – is understood to be an expression of the wisdom and spiritual qualities of the central figure. It is as though the main figure of the mandala is like a fountain, pouring outwards, its waters taking on different forms. (Incidentally, one of the most common ways in which we encounter mandala patterns in the West is in formal gardens, with flower beds arranged in careful patterns around a central ornament. In many European gardens I have wanted to remove the ugly plaster Cupid or whatever from the centre, and replace it with something symbolizing a higher reality. Then some of these gardens would become really pleasing shrines.)

It is time to meet the five Buddhas of the mandala. Although we can talk of them as a set of five separate

Buddhas, in a sense there is just one Buddha. The four who surround him emphasize different aspects of the one experience of Enlightenment. They are that total experience seen from four different points of view.

The symbolism associated with each Buddha is very distinctive. In particular each Buddha has a special Wisdom, a vision of Reality which he especially embodies. This is perhaps the most important feature of these figures. Through contemplating these Buddhas we can begin to see life through their eyes and gain a feeling for their Enlightened vision. When you see the world from this perspective, even the most everyday experiences are embraced by that Wisdom. Hence Tantric Buddhism came to connect these five figures symbolically with virtually every aspect of reality, mundane and transcendental. Thus each Buddha traditionally has a host of associations, and I discuss several of the most important ones in the text. You will also find them summarized in a table at the end of the book. (The associations vary according to different traditions. Here I have followed the system of the Nyingma School of Tibetan Buddhism, derived from the text known in English as the *Tibetan Book of the Dead*.)

Trying to connect with the associations – to see why certain aspects of experience should be linked with one Buddha rather than another – is a frustrating but ultimately rewarding exercise. It is frustrating because Tantra is an 'organic' system; the correlations rarely fit into a neat logical scheme. Just when you have four aspects of something neatly assigned to four of the Buddhas, the fifth will often be bafflingly inappropriate. It is ultimately rewarding because reflecting on the correlations can spark off your spiritual intuition.

I am not going to describe the mandala as it appears in the more traditional visualization practices. Rather I am going to treat it in a way which I hope will give more of a feeling for the different Buddhas and the net of symbolism which connects them. The five Buddhas are also known as the five Jinas (conquerors) because they have overcome ignorance and entered the realm of Reality. They are like five spiritual kings, each with his own territory, or Pure Land, over which he holds sway, teaching the Dharma – the eternal truth discovered by Shakyamuni. We will visit first the kingdom in the East....

2

AKSHOBHYA: THE IMPERTURBABLE

AKSHOBHYA IS SEATED at the heart of his realm, on a vast blue lotus throne, supported by four massive elephants. The Buddha's body is made of deep blue light, the colour of the night sky in the tropics. He has dark hair, is dressed in flowing, richly ornamented robes, and sits in the full-lotus posture. He is smiling, and his whole body radiates light. His left hand rests in his lap, totally relaxed. Standing upright on its palm is a golden vajra.

His right hand reaches down, palm inwards. The tips of the deep blue fingers just touch the white moon mat on which he sits. There is something about the gesture which speaks to you. It is coming home, it is hitting the bedrock of existence, it is the answer to all questions. His whole figure conveys unshakeable confidence. He is so rooted that nothing could ever ruffle his composure. In understanding the meaning of his gesture all the inhabitants of his realm become wise, and enter a stage of the path to Enlightenment from which there is no falling back.

In his heart is a syllable, made of pale blue light. It is the syllable *hum*, symbol of the integration of the individual and the universal. From his heart echoes the mantra which embodies his Wisdom. Its sound carries everywhere in his realm, slow and measured, like the call of a great drum: *om ... vajra ... Akshobhya ... hum*.

The sound of the *hum* has all the unshakeable certainty with which an elephant places its foot upon the earth. It has the same unalterable quality as the Buddha's fingers touching the ground. It is a stamp, a seal of Reality, just as an action in a moment of time, once the moment is past, can never be erased or undone.

Seeing and hearing all this, your mind becomes absolutely tranquil and steady. Each moment is a total experience, which you feel in its full weight and depth. It lacks nothing; it is complete as it is. Everything is just a perfect reflection in the mirror of your mind.

In one account, from the Mahayana (Great Way) school of Buddhism, Shakyamuni Buddha describes Akshobhya's history. Ages ago, in a land called Abhirati (intense delight) a Buddha called Vishalaksha was faced with a monk who wanted to vow to gain Enlightenment for the sake of all living beings. The Buddha warned him that he would be undertaking a daunting task, as to attain his goal he would have to forswear all feelings of anger. In response, the monk took a series of great vows: never to give way to anger or bear malice, never to engage in the slightest immoral action, and many others. Over aeons he was unshakeable (*'akshobhya'* in Sanskrit) in holding to his vow, and as a result he became a Buddha of that name.

Perhaps the best-known text in which Akshobhya appears is the *Perfection of Wisdom in 8,000 Lines*. He is a particularly important figure in the Tantras, because like all Buddhas of the mandala he does not stand alone; he is head of a kula or 'family' of spiritual figures.

Akshobhya's spiritual family is called the Vajra family. The vajra is the symbolic diamond thunderbolt. In the last chapter we found a wall of vajras encircling the mandala. Akshobhya has a single vajra, as a diamond sceptre, standing upright in his left palm. It is an emblem of sovereignty which is held by Indra, the king of the gods in Indian tradition. However, it is far more than just a sign of kingship.

The schoolboy riddle 'what happens when an irresistible force meets an immovable object?' has been answered by Tantric Buddhism. It just fused the two together to make the vajra. The vajra has all the immutable qualities of a diamond – so strong that nothing can cut it or make an impression on it. At the same time it is an irresistible force. It is an Eastern relative of the thunderbolt wielded by Zeus and Athena in the Greek myths, and of the hammer of Thor, the storm god of Norse mythology. It is the thunderbolt which can smash anything that crosses its path.

For Buddhism, it is transcendental reality that has these irresistible, immutable qualities. Everything mundane is mutable and changing. So the vajra becomes a symbol for Reality and, by extension, for the intuitive wisdom that realizes it.

The stylized vajra used in Tantric ritual has four main parts. At its centre is an egg shape, representing the primordial unity of all things before they 'fall' into dualism. Emerging from either side of the egg shape are lotus flowers. With them is born the world of opposites, including the opposition between samsara – the endless cycle of mundane existence – and nirvana – the state of Enlightenment. From each of the lotuses protrudes the head of a strange animal, a makara. This is a kind of crocodile, whose amphibious nature hints at a meeting of conscious heights and unconscious depths. Then each end of the vajra branches out into a number of prongs. Usually there are four at each end, which finally reunite at the vajra's tip. Running vertically through the whole vajra is another prong. So if one looks at the end of a vajra what one sees is a mandala arrangement, usually with four spokes around a central point.

It is understood that one end of the vajra stands for the negative qualities that chain us to samsara, the other for the spiritual qualities that free us. The great achievement of the Tantra is that its perspective is broad enough to unite the two. So the same axis runs through both mandalas. For the Tantra even negative forces such as hatred or envy are seen simply as the pure play of Reality. Furthermore, it suggests that there are correlations between negative qualities and Enlightened ones. Redirected, the energies tied up in greed, pride, and other unskilful states can be used to fuel our pursuit of Enlightenment.

To make this point as forcefully as possible, the Tantra associated every aspect of the mundane with a spiritual quality. For instance, looking at the table of correlations at the end of this book you will see that Akshobhya is associated not just with wisdom, but also with dawn, water, and even with hatred and the hells.

The Tantra would never sanction hatred directed towards any living being, but hatred can be redirected and used to further our development. When we are experiencing it there is often a kind of clear, cold precision to the way in which we see the faults of things. It is a state completely devoid of sentimentality or vagueness. We just have to see what the real enemy is. Once we hate suffering and ignorance, and are hell-bent on destroying them, that energy leads us to Akshobhya's Pure Land rather than into the hells of violence and despair.

To examine all the different correlations with each of the five Buddhas would make this book very long indeed. I have hinted at some of them in describing their realms, others you can see and reflect on in the table of associations. It is enough that we see the idea: that for the Tantra everything is a reminder, even an expression, of Reality. Dawn, blueness, even a glass of water, can all bring to mind Akshobhya. When you see everything in this way, the ordinary world of appearances starts to become a Pure Land.

Now that we have learned a little about Akshobhya and the vajra, it is time to answer a question: how did Akshobhya appear? There is a strong connection between one of Akshobhya's qualities and a particular incident in Shakyamuni's life, known as the incident of 'calling the Earth Goddess to witness'.

Legend describes the historical Buddha seated under his tree, striving to gain Enlightenment through profound meditation. The tremendous force of his effort soon drew the attention of Mara. Mara is the personification in Buddhism of everything mundane, everything either inside or outside ourselves which binds us to the wheel of conditioned existence. His name literally means Death. The last thing Mara wanted was anyone escaping from his realm by gaining Enlightenment, so he launched an all-out attack on the meditating figure. He sent powerful armies against the Buddha. They deluged him with boulders and weapons. Yet he continued tranquilly meditating, and all the rocks, spears, and arrows, as soon as they touched the aura of peaceful concentration around him, just turned to flowers which rained down at his feet. Having failed to shift him by force, Mara sent his daughters to try to seduce him. But the Buddha did not even look at them. He just continued his inward search for freedom.

After these crude assaults had failed, Mara tried something trickier. He approached the Buddha and said, 'You are sitting on the seat on which all the Buddhas of old gained Enlightenment. By what right do you sit on that seat?' Legend has it that all Buddhas gain Enlightenment on the same spot, the *vajrasana* (diamond seat), which is the first point to solidify out of the swirling gases at the beginning of universal evolution, and will be the last point to dissolve away at its end.

The Buddha replied, 'I have practised generosity, ethical discipline, and other spiritual practices for aeons, so I have earned the right to take my place here.' But Mara pretended not to be satisfied. He said to the Buddha, 'You may say that, but who is your witness?'

The answer to Mara was emphatic. The Buddha said nothing. With the fingertips of his right hand, he just touched the earth. In response, out of the ground in front of him sprang the goddess of the Earth. The Earth Goddess said, 'I will be his witness. I have seen him purifying himself for aeons through spiritual practices.' This was the Buddha's answer. With it he finally put paid to Mara's efforts to deter him. He continued his meditation unhindered, and at last gained supreme and perfect Enlightenment.

It was perhaps through meditating on this incident in the legendary life of the historical Buddha that Buddhist yogins and yoginis made contact with the Buddha Akshobhya. Dwelling on the qualities he exhibited, seeing them at their most potent, they came upon Akshobhya. When he answers Mara by touching the earth, Shakyamuni is pointing to the fact that he is ready to gain Enlightenment because the seeds of all the positive actions he has performed during aeons on the spiritual path are now going to come to fruition.

He calls as his witness the Earth Goddess, who rises up from the depths of his consciousness. The Earth faithfully preserves the marks of everything that happens upon it. Working down through its strata you can reconstruct its history. Every action has had its effect.

The Earth is dumb witness to the lives and struggles of all human beings. It bears the scars of their building and destruction. It harbours their dust when the day is over.

Akshobhya makes the same earth-touching mudra, the same gesture expressing the quality of unshakeability, as Shakyamuni did when challenged by Mara. Seeing how the symbolism of Akshobhya is connected with this aspect of the historical Buddha's Enlightenment experience, I begin to wonder about Akshobhya's symbolic animals. Is it really just a coincidence that the 'royal beasts' of the eastern realm are elephants, who it is claimed 'never forget'? While that may just be a prank of nature, what is certain is that we still have one more step to take in unfolding the significance of the earth-touching mudra.

To do this we need to consider the symbolism of the elements in relation to Akshobhya. With his rooted immutable quality, as he sits on his elephant throne, touching the earth, you might confidently assume that the element associated with Akshobhya is earth. However, it is water. After you have been contemplating the mandala of the five Buddhas for a while, this will come as no surprise. As I suggested in the last chapter, the mandala possesses an organic unity which goes deeper than the rational. Trying to fit together all the connections into a logical scheme is like trying to cram a large elephant into a somewhat smaller packing case. There is always some part which will not quite fit in.

Nonetheless, there is a rational explanation for Akshobhya's association with water. This brings us on to the most important quality of the five Buddhas. Each of them embodies a Wisdom – an Enlightened way of seeing. This is their prime message. Meditating upon them, what we are really trying to do is come to a realization of the Wisdom which is their essential nature.

The special Wisdom to be found in the east, through meeting Akshobhya, is the Mirror-Like Wisdom. With this Wisdom we see everything just as it is, impartially and unaffected. Hold up a red rose to a mirror – or a bloody dagger. It will reflect them both just as they are; it will make no judgements between the two reds, wanting to hold the first and flee from the second. Reality is just our experience, with no ideas added on. The mind perfectly reflects everything, but is not stained by it – just as the still waters of a bay can perfectly reflect a raft or a palace, without feeling any need to choose one above the other. It is this capacity of water to act as mirror which makes it particularly appropriate to Akshobhya.

None of the reflections in a mirror stick to it, none are repelled by it. The mirror never reacts. It always stays imperturbable, immutable. Reaching this stage of practice, producing no new karma, serenely allowing the drama of birth and death to play itself out for the last time, you have entered the Pure Land of Akshobhya. You have seen the deep blue figure of the Immutable Buddha, holding the thunderbolt sceptre of Reality which smashes through all ideas and concepts about it. At the same time the dark blue fingertips of his right hand touch the earth, the earth of direct experience, which is the only thing upon which any of us can finally rely.

Plate 1   THE MANDALA OF THE FIVE BUDDHAS

Plate 2   AKSHOBHYA

Plate 3   RATNASAMBHAVA

Plate 4   AMITABHA

Plate 5 AMOGHASIDDHI

Plate 6   VAIROCHANA

Plate 7   SHAKYAMUNI

Plate 8   CHAKRASAMVARA MANDALA

3

RATNASAMBHAVA: THE JEWEL-BORN

THE YELLOW BUDDHA Ratnasambhava sits on a great
yellow lotus throne, supported by four horses. In his left
hand, which rests in his lap, he holds a beautiful jewel.
His right rests on his right knee, palm outwards, in a
gesture of supreme giving. His generosity is limitless.
He provides everything that the dwellers in his realm
could wish for. Being in his world, you feel an abundance
of energy and creativity, an overflowing happiness. You
feel love and wisdom increasing, like plants growing in
fertile soil.

After the sharp clarity of Akshobhya's dawn, everything has blended into the haze of noon – the time of day
associated with Ratnasambhava. His brilliant light sof-
tens the edges of the landscape's features; everything is
honeyed by his golden radiance. His Wisdom brings out
the common features of experience. It sees all aspects of
life, all the myriad forms it takes, as equally devoid of
any inherent existence. Thus Ratnasambhava is

particularly associated with transforming pride into the Wisdom of Sameness and with the human realm of the Wheel of Life. The Wheel of Life graphically represents the whole of cyclic existence. It portrays all living beings as occupying one of six realms: heavenly beings, jealous titans, humans, animals, hungry ghosts, and hell beings. These can be interpreted literally, as six different realms into which one may be born, or psychologically, as different mental states – all of which are experienced by human beings. Ratnasambhava sees the 'common humanity' in all beings and cares for them all equally.

As well as 'Jewel-Born', Ratnasambhava's name could also be translated 'the Jewel-Producing One'. He is associated with riches, and is sometimes described as the Buddha of Giving. Being infinitely rich, he makes no distinctions of worth, giving freely to all. All beings are equally precious. After all, Ratnasambhava is associated with the element earth, and earth is the great leveller. Whatever our social position, whatever our race or sex, whatever our life form even, we are all made from the common clay. The golden sunlight of Ratnasambhava shines equally on palace and dung-heap. Through contacting his Wisdom we develop a solidarity with all forms of life.

Ratnasambhava's qualities bring to mind several images suggestive of pride being levelled, and the assertion of what all life has in common. There is Shelley's sonnet 'Ozymandias', in which he meets a traveller who tells him of coming upon the remains of a vast statue in the desert. The inscription on the pedestal reads:

My name is Ozymandias, king of kings:
Look on my works, ye Mighty, and despair!

The statue is a total ruin. As the traveller wryly observes:

Nothing beside remains. Round the decay
Of that colossal wreck, boundless and bare
The lone and level sands stretch far away.

Then there is the Midas myth. King Midas is a sad caricature of Ratnasambhava. He too is associated with both riches and equality. Everything he touches turns to gold. However, he destroys the humanity of things; even his family and food turn to gold at his touch. His avarice estranges him from the human realm. His power of wealth becomes a torment for him.

The Wisdom of Sameness gives equanimity. We experience the 'eight worldly winds' – gain and loss, fame and disgrace, praise and blame, pleasure and pain – as equals, knowing that to chase one will be to lay ourselves open to the other. As we learn to treat each of these 'two impostors' with calm impartiality, they lose their hold over us. We become like the earth, which receives all equally. We can do this only if we cease to relate to things personally, seeing their advantages and disadvantages for us. To do this we need to find one more aspect of sameness: the equality of ourselves and others. The Wisdom of Sameness is not a cold meting out of equal justice. It is a strong positive identification with all life. Ratnasambhava's golden light dissolves the boundaries of self and other. When those disappear, all sense of property and ownership vanishes. Then you just share with others – without even any sense of giving, because giving requires a 'self' to give and 'others' to receive.

Ratnasambhava's emblem is the jewel, and he is head of the Ratna (or Jewel) family. With his gesture of supreme giving (the *varada* mudra), open palm turned outward, he showers the world with precious things. For people in the West who have cut their teeth on consumerism and materialism, he offers a familiar-looking and attractive gateway to the Dharma.

However, you may be wondering what this has to do with Buddhism. Ratnasambhava is a fully Enlightened Buddha. There has to be more to his practice than getting rich on the Stock Market. So let us look at the different levels on which the symbolism of wealth can be understood.

On the most basic level, a Buddha wants to relieve people's suffering, even their everyday suffering. So if wealth will make them temporarily happy, then let them be given wealth. In his *Entering the Path of Enlightenment* (Sanskrit *Bodhicharyavatara*), the great Buddhist poet Shantideva says: 'For all creatures, I would be a lantern for those desiring a lantern, I would be a bed for those desiring a bed, a slave for those desiring a slave.'

However, in reflecting on Ratnasambhava one begins to obtain some of his spiritual riches – he is very generous with them. Dwelling on his shining yellow figure, with its jewel in one hand and mudra of giving, one begins to feel a greater expansiveness in oneself. The essential change he can bring about is a shift from a poverty mentality to a wealth mentality.

All too often we are concerned in our lives with a sense of lack. We do not have enough money, are not attractive enough, need a bigger house, and so on. Once we move on to a spiritual path, the blaring demands of our physical wants begin to subside. We are prepared to live a simpler life. However, we usually still feel a sense of lack, now transferred to the spiritual plane. This is what Chögyam Trungpa Rimpoche called 'spiritual materialism'. Still with our sense of lack, we go in search of more blissful meditations, a more famous guru, a more powerful teaching.

But we are still looking in the wrong place for satisfaction. We are still driven by an inner poverty to find some external riches to fill us. Reflecting on Ratnasambhava changes this feeling. We see him pouring spiritual riches endlessly upon the universe, without a moment's thought for the possibility of running out of reserves. He is the ceaseless benefactor, patron, philanthropist, host. Because his source of riches is unconditioned Enlightenment, he has access to an infinite reservoir of spiritual energy. So the thought of being careful, of hoarding what he has, rationing and allocating priorities, never occurs in his Pure Land, called 'the Glorious'. Everything in his realm flows in abundance. He is rich 'beyond the dreams of avarice'.

Through developing on the path of Ratnasambhava we soon feel no material lack. We realize that the higher world of the spiritual can give us the endless satisfaction which a Mercedes and a penthouse flat never could. Our own mind is a source of endless riches. As our develop-

ment continues we mine deeper within ourselves, and
from the ore of our direct experience we smelt more and
more precious qualities.

The poison associated with Ratnasambhava is pride.
However, pride is one side of a duality of which the other
is always present. Where you have pride and a conscious
over-valuation of yourself, hidden in the basement of
your psyche is a great deal of insecurity. Similarly, within
every Uriah Heep there is usually a well-concealed ego-
tist to be found. Ratnasambhava's Wisdom of Sameness
shows us that whether we play high status or low the
result is still the same. We are still too much concerned
with ourselves.

He also shows us the way out. He is supremely generous, and it is not possible truly to give without awareness of others. Giving takes you beyond yourself. It
involves seeing the needs of others, and what will satisfy
those needs. Through awareness of others we enter the
human realm, which as we have seen is the realm of the
Wheel of Life over which Ratnasambhava presides.

The human realm is the realm of co-operation. Here
you come into relation with others, and no longer feel
the isolation of pride. It is the only realm in which you
can naturally feel the support of others, and hence escape both pride and lack of self-esteem. It is also the only
realm in which you can empathize with others. Empa-
thizing with them, you become rich in their riches. So it
is the world of 'rejoicing in merits' – appreciating the
good qualities of others and rejoicing in their happiness
– of which Ratnasambhava seems to be the patron.

Ratnasambhava is associated with aesthetic appreciation, and has been called by one Western teacher the
Buddha of Beauty. This is a very important aspect of
spiritual life. Sages and yogins from the time of the
Buddha onwards have sung songs in appreciation of the
natural beauties of the places where they lived and
meditated. All Buddhist traditions have tried, each in its
own way, to make their shrines, temples, and hermitages
aesthetic and harmonious. Zen temples have their spare,
spacious beauty; Thai temples their sweeping shapes
and gilded pinnacles; Tibetan shrines their profusion of
statues and paintings, sometimes spilling over like an
avalanche of the archetypal into the everyday world.

This beauty and richness is more than an expression of
devotion to the highest values in Buddhism. The contemplation of beauty has a refining and transforming
effect on our emotions, which are often tied up in quite
basic needs and wants. It is not easy to make the emotional leap from enjoying these relatively coarse satisfac-
tions to deriving our emotional sustenance from the
archetypal realm of Buddhas and Bodhisattvas. We need
to wean ourselves gradually off the one and learn to
nourish ourselves with the other. This is where culture
and the appreciation of beauty in nature and the arts has
its place. Through dwelling on natural beauty, or on
great artistic works such as those of Shakespeare, Bach,
Michelangelo, or Raphael, our energies become more
refined. From being human animals, we climb towards
the peak of human achievement from which it is

relatively easy to take the fathomless leap into the sky of Enlightened consciousness.

Ratnasambhava also holds the antidote to a modern Western malady. As competition for jobs and trade becomes fiercer, people in the Western world find it harder just to stop, relax, and do nothing (without turning on the television). We are too 'full of care' to have the time to 'stand and stare'. Boxed in by skyscrapers, we miss out on cloud patterns and stars. Sitting in snarled traffic, late for appointments, we hardly notice our surroundings. However, Ratnasambhava's whole attitude is one of superabundance, including that of time. He encourages us to take the time to experience the world around us, trying to see it through the eyes of his Wisdom of Equality. Then we may have something of the vision of William Blake:

> *To see a world in a grain of sand,*
> *And a heaven in a wild flower,*
> *Hold infinity in the palm of your hand,*
> *And eternity in an hour.*

This surplus of time relates to Ratnasambhava's world being one of artistic creation. From the point of view of human survival, the arts are a luxury. We could exist without music, theatre, novels, or sculpture. They have tended to flower in times of wealth and leisure. (Incidentally, the same is true of spiritual life – India at the time of the Buddha was a wealthy society with a surplus which could feed thousands of wandering ascetics and holy men.)

Ratnasambhava shows us the way to open ourselves up to a wider world. The mandalas of our lives are often constricted, limited by our grim determination to get what we want. We spend most of our time aware of things and people only in terms of their use-value, especially their usefulness to us. Of course we cannot neglect the practicalities of life; we need to get things done. However, if we are to be happy our utilitarian concerns must be allocated a small and not too central place in the mandala of our life. The greater part of our mandala should be reserved for aesthetic appreciation, in which we value things for what they are in themselves.

The difference between these two attitudes is well exemplified by the reactions of two visitors to London early in the nineteenth century. The poet Wordsworth, standing on Westminster Bridge early one morning in the summer of 1802, wrote the famous sonnet beginning:

Earth has not anything to show more fair;
Dull would he be of soul who could pass by
A sight so touching in its majesty.

A decade later the Prussian field-marshal Blücher, surveying the same city, was moved to exclaim 'What a place to plunder!'

Ratnasambhava, then, encourages us to develop more aesthetic appreciation of life. A good way to work at this is regularly to set aside time to contemplate some kind of natural beauty. Part of the reason people relax in natural surroundings is that, as well as being peaceful and visually pleasing, they do not stimulate the tendency to utilitarianism. You cannot use or possess a sunset; you can only appreciate its beauty and allow it to enrich your spirit.

Taking this a little further, we could also associate Ratnasambhava with ecology and environmental concern. He is connected with the earth, fertility, and the flourishing abundance of life. Also it is he who holds the antidote to pride, and it is the hubris of the human race which is causing irreparable damage to our beautiful planet. His wisdom can teach us to aesthetically appreciate the Earth, rather than constantly looking for new ways to exploit it.

This superabundance of Ratnasambhava leads us to associate him with another quality which has connections with aesthetic appreciation. That quality is playfulness. Play is a sign of spare energy, and of a wider perspective than is needed for the task in hand. It is creativity without any object in view beyond itself. As such, it can be a celebration of human consciousness. The energy that pours from Ratnasambhava, the ebullience of spiritual riches, gives us free energy and an expansive, relaxed vision. Out of this we can play – without needing any reason or justification.

Something of this abundance of energy is symbolized by Ratnasambhava's animal, the horse. The horse is an animal that can be tamed to become docile and obedient to the human. It puts all its raw energy under the direction of a human consciousness. On a deeper level, the horse is a symbol for the subtle energies within the human body that can be brought under control and refined through meditation. This symbolism is embodied in the figure of the windhorse. The windhorse is shown in Buddhist iconography as a kind of messenger, a little like Pegasus, the winged horse of Greek mythology. Though he has no wings the windhorse flies through the air, carrying on his back the precious burden of the Three Jewels – the Buddha, the Dharma, and the Sangha (spiritual community).

To close this chapter, we need to look once more at the jewel that Ratnasambhava holds. Although it can be related to the appreciation of beauty, and the pouring of the wealth of the Three Jewels upon the world, there is a further level to its symbolism. The jewel the yellow Buddha holds is a wish-fulfilling jewel, the chintamani – the jewel that gives you all you could wish for. In Buddhism it became a symbol for the Bodhichitta – the compassion that impels us to gain Enlightenment for the sake of all living beings.

It is as though Buddhism says, 'You have been searching all through your life for fulfilment, in money, sex, companionship, success, and so on. Your intuition that complete happiness is possible is correct; you've just been looking in the wrong place, among impermanent phenomena. What you have been looking for all along, intuitively, is the Bodhichitta. When you have that you have everything. All your desires will be fulfilled by that experience.'

Having found the real wish-fulfilling gem, the experience of Enlightened Compassion, we shall feel totally satisfied. Then all we shall want to do is share with others the limitless spiritual riches we have found. So the first of the Perfections is generosity, and this is the main spiritual practice of someone in whom the Bodhi-chitta has arisen. That person is prepared to give any-thing to help others.

If we too practise the perfection of generosity we will not hold back from giving lest we are left with nothing. We will happily give ourselves completely. Then we will find that we have gained the whole world. We will have inherited the inexhaustible riches of Ratnasambhava.

4

AMITABHA: INFINITE LIGHT

NEXT WE TURN to the red Buddha, Amitabha, whose name means 'Infinite Light'. Amitabha is a glowing warm red, with curly blue-black hair. He is always seated in the full-lotus posture, and generally his hands are in the meditation mudra, though occasionally he may be holding up a red lotus in his right hand. He is dressed in deep red ornately embroidered robes. Around his head is usually a glowing green aura, and around his body a red one. Both are edged with rainbows.

Sometimes he is seen seated on a deep red lotus which floats on a calm ocean, so that his radiant form – like a setting sun – casts a path of light across the waters. Through repeatedly dwelling on this we can absorb the glowing warmth of love and compassion that radiates from Amitabha. Our mind gradually acquires something of his oceanic depth of feeling. We become like the great ocean, with a warm centre of unfailing love at our heart; the restless waves of thought all stilled.

For Indo-Tibetan Buddhism red is the colour of love and compassion, and of the whole emotional aspect of life. Amitabha, then, is the Buddha of Love and Compassion. As such, he is totally approachable. His time of day is sunset, and his direction the west. So he is like the setting sun. Sunset is a miracle; you can look directly into the fierce power of the sun, and it is gentle and causes you no harm. As it disappears into the west the sun is like a proud and fierce king, who at the end of the day's hunting turns gentle and jovial, and allows anyone to approach him. (Also the setting sun may suggest the withdrawal of the light of consciousness from the world of the senses as it turns within to higher states of meditative concentration.)

The spiritual power of Amitabha is all warmth and gentleness. He is the colour of ruby. His colour is the most striking, the first colour recognized by children. He is the colour of fascination. He is the colour of blood; he is the blushing colour of delicate emotion, the suffusing shade of emotional arousal. Through him, all one's emotional energy is gently led into the quest for Enlightenment.

The poison with which he is associated is *raga* – passion. The nature of passion is that it attaches itself strongly to a particular object. Meditating on Amitabha arouses emotional energy, but transmutes mundane passion into Discriminating Wisdom. This is the counterbalance to the Wisdom of Equality of Ratnasambhava, which saw the common factor in all changing appearances. The Wisdom of Amitabha sees the uniqueness, the distinctive characteristics, of every phenomenon.

A passionate lover wants just to be with the one unique, seemingly irreplaceable, person who is the object of their love. They are highly aware of that person's distinctive qualities. Small things about them are endearing: a particular mannerism, a way of moving the head, a typical phrase. All these are special and lovable because they are signs, distinguishing marks, of the loved one. Similarly, the Discriminating Wisdom of Amitabha sees and loves the minute differences in things. The distinction between the lover's appreciation and Amitabha's Wisdom is that Discriminating Wisdom is non-dual. It introduces no idea of self and other. Hence it does not make its loving appreciation of uniqueness into a basis for exclusive attachment.

Amitabha's special emblem is the lotus, and he is head of the Lotus family. He is thus associated with all the attributes of the lotus: gentleness, openness, and the more 'receptive' qualities. The quality of openness is further stressed by his element, fire, which consumes everything, creating space. Even more so, the totality of his openness is reflected in a legend associated with his heraldic animal, the peacock. According to myth, peacocks are capable of swallowing poisonous snakes without coming to harm. This symbolism, of being open even to poison, and transmuting it into beauty (as the snake nourishes the peacock's beautiful plumage) is very striking. It gives us a feeling for the transforming power of Amitabha's love and compassion. On an everyday level, this legend suggests that even our darkest and most venomous aspects can be transformed by practising the Dharma.

The realm of the Wheel of Life which Amitabha transmutes is that of the hungry ghosts. These are beings whose lives are spent in frustrated craving. They are usually represented with large stomachs and tiny mouths. Amitabha's love dissolves away the feelings of desperation and being unloved and unlovable which cause them to grab at life. His power of meditation takes them away from their restless and unfulfilled state on to a deeper and more satisfying level of themselves.

In general, the path to Enlightenment represented by Amitabha is the reverse of Akshobhya's. The approach of the Vajra family is more overtly dynamic. Through it you become increasingly vajric, breaking through obstacles, hurtling towards Enlightenment. The approach of Amitabha is more 'organic'. Gently and gradually you unfold the petals of your spiritual potential until you ripen into Enlightenment. The path of Akshobhya, transmuting hatred, is one of aversion to samsara, the mundane world permeated with suffering. Amitabha's path is one of attraction to nirvana, the longing desire to embrace that warm red sun.

Amitabha also has a reflex form – Amitayus. *Ayus* means life in Sanskrit, so Amitayus is 'Infinite Life'. He is particularly associated with practices for gaining longevity. Whilst Amitabha is usually represented holding a begging-bowl, Amitayus holds a precious vase, full of the nectar of immortality. The two figures Infinite Light and Infinite Life clearly represent the same principle viewed from the points of view of space and time respectively. Indeed, Indian Buddhism seems to treat Amitabha and Amitayus as the same figure, and it is only in the Tantric Buddhism of Tibet and Japan that one finds them regarded as separate.

Though it is simple, Amitabha's figure has an archetypal quality to it. He is a meditating Buddha, with his hands in the *dhyana* mudra – the mudra of meditation. When people without any special interest in Buddhism think about it, it is this image that frequently comes to mind. The meditating Buddha can now be found in many places in the West: in museums and galleries, in books and junk shops. (I have even seen one turned into a lampstand.)

The meditating Buddha is the central image of Buddhism, arising out of the crucial experience of the entire Buddhist tradition: the Buddha's attainment of Enlightenment whilst seated in deep meditation under the bodhi tree. One should be able to tell a great deal about a spiritual tradition just by contemplating its central symbol. Surprisingly, I think this is particularly true if you just contemplate the image, without any explanation of its supposed meaning within the tradition. (For example, contemplating a crucifix, purely as an image, can tell you a great deal about the nature of Christianity.) The meditating Buddha, the central symbol of Buddhism, is, I think, part of the reason why Buddhism enjoys a good reputation in the West. People are often well disposed to Buddhism because, without their necessarily being very conscious of it, the meditating Buddha image has deeply affected them.

If you look at a meditating Buddha figure, in stone, bronze, brass, plaster, wood, or whatever, you pick up certain impressions from it. Its posture is regular, well-balanced, pleasing. It has a solidity about it. It is upright and immovable. It doesn't worry or bite its nails. It is centred. In fact it looks almost as though it had put down roots into the earth.

The figure just sits, silent, contented. He has no appointments to make, no train to catch. He is peaceful, calm, welcoming. If you have a few minutes to sit with him and join him in meditation, before you have to rush off, he will be pleased.

He is timeless. He could sit there for ever. Some of the old stone Buddhas seem to have been sitting silently, deepening their concentration, for a thousand years or more. The Buddhas at Nalanda in India have meditated steadily through changing fortunes. First covered in garlands and cared for by devoted monks, then suffering patiently as Muslim invaders beat at them with sticks, now they are still rapt in concentration while planes fly overhead and tourists wander by.

There is something awe-inspiring about a meditating Buddha. What is he gazing at deep within, with that faint smile of knowledge on his lips? One feels he has dived into an endless inner ocean, to find the sunken treasures of the universe, the rubies of the mind.

A figure in the meditation posture can be awe-inspiring whether made of stone or of flesh and blood. A story is told of Daito, a Zen master, who for a while lived with beggars under the bridges of Kyoto. In those days it was the brutal custom for a samurai to test a new sword on a human victim. One evening a samurai was seen roaming the area with a new sword. The beggars were terrified as they knew that after dark the samurai would come to test his sword on one of their 'expendable' number. Daito told them all to hide. Then he sat himself calmly in the meditation posture on the road. Night fell. The samurai came along, and saw an unmoving victim. He cried out to Daito to prepare to die, as he was going to cleave him in two with his sword. There was no reply. The calm figure sat in front of him, giving off that feeling of vast, gently harnessed energy which comes from someone in deep meditation. Looking at his serene victim, the samurai faltered, unnerved. Finally he slunk away into the night.

Let us come back to contemplating Amitabha, our meditating Buddha. Look at his hands. They are joined, one hand resting on the other, thumbs lightly touching, placed near the centre of his body. What can they tell us? They speak of how relaxed he is. They express the union of opposites. They are both active and receptive. The thumbs just touch. With less exertion they would not meet, with more they would press upwards and break the perfect oval formed by the hands. They are suggestive of the Middle Way and the Buddha's advice to Sona. Sona was a monk who practised walking meditation for so long, pacing up and down, that his feet bled. The Buddha explained to him how in his meditation he should be like a well-tuned lute. If the strings are either too slack or too tight it cannot be played. The gently-touching thumbs maintain a constant awareness of a balanced spiritual development.

We have looked at the hands but we have yet to consider the most important aspect of the mudra. What we have not looked at is the oval space enclosed between the palms and the arch of the thumbs. Amitabha, like all meditating Buddhas, embraces space as his most precious possession. That empty space is like an egg, an egg of Emptiness which the meditating Buddha sits patiently 'incubating'. What will be hatched from it? A Buddha's only concern is to create conditions which will be helpful for living beings to escape from suffering. So from the egg of Emptiness an entire Pure Land will emerge, with its infinite radiance and inexhaustible Dharma teachings.

It is through the power of his meditation on infinite love and compassion that Amitabha brings into existence his Pure Land. However, even love and compassion would not be enough to create this greatest of all masterpieces of the mind. It is only when combined with an understanding of Emptiness, of the insubstantial nature of all phenomena, that Amitabha's feelings for all beings can create a world for them to live in.

Watching Amitabha creating a Pure Land through his mental power should raise a question in our minds. If a Buddha creates a mental world, is the situation any different for ordinary beings such as us? The general answer of Buddhism seems to be that we are creating our world all the time – not a Pure Land, but a world which is pure or impure depending on our volitions.

Contemplating the serene figure of our meditating Buddha we can understand more clearly what is at stake in meditation practice. We learn the lesson of that oval of space he cradles in the meditation mudra. It is through the spacious awareness we can create in meditation, space to look at how our thoughts create a world, that we can change *our* world. When we see that we do create our world we can begin to take responsibility for it, and then work to create a new world for ourselves by raising our level of consciousness, creating worlds of greater and greater happiness and beauty.

5

AMOGHASIDDHI:
UNOBSTRUCTED SUCCESS

THE BUDDHA OF the northern realm is Amoghasiddhi, whose name means 'Unobstructed Success'. Of all Buddha figures he is perhaps the most mysterious and ungraspable. He is a dark green figure clad in scarlet robes, who is often depicted moving rapidly through space. His attributes and emblems are redolent of power and energy, yet his activity is subtle and hidden. He appears out of the vast expanse of sky, but a deep velvet blue sky of midnight in the tropics.

In his left hand sits a double vajra, a sceptre made of two crossed diamond thunderbolts. As we saw when we met Akshobhya, the single vajra is a symbol of awesome power and force. It can cut through anything whilst always remaining unaffected. Nothing mundane can withstand its impact. The double vajra has all these qualities reinforced.

The double vajra is a symbol of total psychic integration, of the unfoldment of all potential, of perfect harmony, balance, and equilibrium. It can only be encountered when one has journeyed into the most profound depths of existence. It can only appear out of the midnight sky of the deepest unconscious. Seen against the deep blue sky, one feels it to be the primordial pattern of human consciousness. It is the perfect ground plan, the potential which we try falteringly and semiconsciously to unfold in our lives.

Not only is it the ground, the blueprint, for human consciousness, it is also, according to Indian Buddhist cosmology, the support on which the universe rests. Buddhist cosmology has a vision every bit as expansive as modern astronomy. It sees universes evolving and passing out of existence over the aeons. The entire universe with its world systems is said to have as its foundation an inconceivably large double vajra.

It has been suggested that this vision of the basis of the cosmos being a double vajra could even have been an attempt to describe something of the same vision of the universe as that of modern science. If you were a Buddhist yogin or yogini, and in the depths of your meditation you went beyond the individual to the universal, and witnessed the passing of aeons, with galaxies appearing and disappearing, how could you describe it? Buddhist cosmology has managed to do it, in terms that we can recognize.

Then what if your mind encompassed even the birth of the universe, the big bang that precipitated our

cosmos into being? How could you describe that un-
thinkable explosion? Perhaps the nearest description
you could find would be that the whole universe was
founded on a vast double thunderbolt, its energies pouring outward from a central point.

Regardless of whether or not the double vajra has any
connection with the big bang, we can draw a profound
lesson from its symbolism. The double vajra supports
the universe. It also forms the deepest pattern in the
midnight depths of our own psyche. So the fundamental
matrix of both the universe and of every individual
consciousness within it is the same. In their common
depths the individual and the universal interpenetrate.
To understand yourself, in your deepest nature, is to
understand the nature of the universe.

Thus the symbolism of the double vajra suggests the
interpenetration, even the fusion, of different levels of
existence. In it, thunderbolts intersect, diamond cuts
diamond and they fuse together. In the double vajra all
opposites unite. With this interpenetration and union of
opposites comes total psychic balance, and integration.

The symbolism of the union of opposites extends beyond the double vajra into Amoghasiddhi's other attributes. He is pulled through space by strange winged
creatures. In Indian Buddhism the animals of Amoghasiddhi are usually garudas – mythical royal birds. However, in Tibetan iconography the garudas transformed
themselves into shang-shang creatures – half man, half
bird – a fusion of human and animal. In *Foundations of
Tibetan Mysticism*, Lama Govinda says of Amoghasiddhi:

*This Inner Way leads into the mystery of Amoghasiddhi:
in which the inner and the outer world, the visible and
the invisible, are united; and in which the spiritual takes
bodily shape, and the body becomes an exponent of the
spirit. For Amoghasiddhi is the lord of the great
transformation, whose vehicle is the winged man, the man
in transition towards a new dimension of consciousness.*

Not only are the shang-shang birds themselves a union
of opposites, but as they fly through space they clash
together cymbals, forcefully uniting all poles of existence.

The symbolism of hybrid creatures is quite a common
one in Buddhism. According to legend, for a short period
after the time of Shakyamuni Buddha's Enlightenment
all hatred in the world ceased. During that time animals
who were natural foes mated to produce animals with
qualities that are antipathetic in the natural world.

It is this fusion of opposites that gives Amoghasiddhi
his mysterious quality. It is really only possible to speak
of him in the language of paradox and contradiction. As
we shall see, he is particularly associated with energy
and action, yet that action is based on the completeness
of the double vajra, which leaves no feeling of need to
act, no volition. He is, in a sense, the most active and
outward-going of the five Buddhas (e.g. he is associated
with the five sense consciousnesses, which apprehend
the external world), yet his activity springs from the
encounter with the double vajra in the innermost depths
of consciousness.

Thus the effects of meditating on Amoghasiddhi seem
to be subtle and hard to grasp. You may not notice much

external change for a while, yet deep down in your being the energies of your psyche are being led into the harmonious patterning called forth by the double vajra. This acts as a form of mandala which, as we have seen, tends to order our energies like iron filings around a magnet. Deep conflicts begin to resolve. Energy is released, but as from a secret spring.

Contemplating the green Buddha you may come to see the world in a more complex, less one-sided way. You begin to understand the practical paradoxes of the spiritual life. You see that to help others is to help yourself. You cannot develop spiritually yourself without helping others to do so. Also, to complete any aspect of development is to begin a new phase. You cannot develop true wisdom without compassion, or vice versa. But, above all else, Amoghasiddhi gradually shows you how self and other, individual and universal, fuse in the diamond-hard centre of the double thunderbolt.

One of the most striking things about the figure of Amoghasiddhi is the power of the gesture he makes with his right hand. It is turned outwards, at the level of his heart, fingers pointing skyward. It is a gesture of command and authority, the *abhaya* mudra or 'gesture of fearlessness'. Amoghasiddhi's whole presence removes terror and fear. His body is green, the colour of the peace and tranquillity of nature. Green is soothing and relaxing, and calms anxiety.

It is easy to find examples of fearlessness in Shakyamuni's life story which could have led people to Amoghasiddhi. There was once a time when threats had been made on the Buddha's life. During the night he emerged from his hut to find monks with sticks standing guard to protect him. He just told them 'a Buddha needs no protection', and sent them away.

On another occasion the Buddha's cousin, Devadatta, in a fit of jealousy, bribed someone to let loose a wild elephant against the Buddha. We can imagine the scene: people scattering in all directions; Devadatta perhaps hidden somewhere out of harm's way where he could watch events; the great beast rushing, maddened, towards the one still figure in a mud-dyed yellow robe. It is an extraordinary contrast. The elephant out of control, head tossing, trunk waving, furious; the Buddha still, erect, serene.

As the beast came towards him, the Buddha suffused it with *maitri*, loving-kindness. Nothing could have entered that enchanted circle of love around the Buddha and maintained thoughts of violence. The mad elephant discovered it was bearing down on the best friend it had in the world. Gradually its charge slowed to a walk, and it reached the Buddha docile and friendly. In this incident we could say that elephant met elephant, for the Buddha was often described as being like a great elephant because of his calm dignity and steady gaze. Perhaps elephant met elephant in a deeper sense too. The Buddha, having gone far beyond dualistic modes of thought, did not feel himself a separate, threatened identity opposed by the huge creature bearing down upon him. His *maitri* came from a total feeling for, and identification with, the charging animal.

These incidents show the Buddha dealing fearlessly with trouble coming his way, but on some occasions the Buddha deliberately put himself in perilous situations in order to help people. Perhaps the best-known example of this is to be found in the story of Angulimala, whose name means 'Garland of Fingers'. Angulimala had taken a vow to kill a hundred people. From each victim he hacked a finger and added it to a gruesome necklace. At the time of the Buddha's arrival in the vicinity, Angulimala's finger total had nearly reached a hundred. He was ferocious, and had terrorized the whole area. No one could withstand him. The Buddha was given a solemn warning about travelling into his domain. He immediately took a route which would bring him close to the assassin's lair.

Angulimala saw the figure of the monk walking quietly along, reached for his sword, and rushed after the Buddha. However, although he was fit and strong, and was running full pelt while the Buddha was mindfully walking, Angulimala could not catch up with him. He redoubled his efforts, but still the steady paces outdistanced him.

Finally, exhausted and baffled, Angulimala cried out 'Stop, monk!' The Buddha's calm reply was 'I have stopped, Angulimala.' The Buddha's mind had stopped dealing in craving, hatred, and ignorance, and had arrived at a place that Angulimala could not reach with his sword. Angulimala was so impressed that he become a disciple of the Buddha on the spot.

This last incident contains several echoes of the symbolism of Amoghasiddhi. There is the fearlessness of the Buddha, there is his active approach in going to find Angulimala, there is the mystery and paradox of how the Buddha, strolling, always outdistances the rushing cutthroat. Amoghasiddhi can show us how true fearlessness is to be attained. Ultimately it can come only from insight into Reality. At that point we realize the illusoriness of the ego we fear for. In particular, fear of dying, the primary fear of which all others are reflections, disappears. There is no one to die.

The double vajra reminds us that fearlessness comes from a full and balanced development of all sides of ourselves. Without that, we shall always have a weak side, a vulnerability that we fear for, and keep having to protect. Even more, we shall have an unexplored aspect, an area of uncharted terrain within, whose characteristics we may experience, projected on to the outside world, as people and situations that are unpredictable and threatening.

It is all too easy to keep developing one's strengths, and to try to make use of them in all situations. Some people even manage to become totally identified with a single talent or a powerful position. From a spiritual point of view this is dangerous. If you wanted to defend a castle, you would not work to make just one or two sides impregnable. Following the Dharma involves developing all aspects of character, all spiritual qualities. This is no easy path to follow, but if we take up the challenge then all the time we are working to overcome our fears the calm, dark green figure of a Buddha will stand by our side, his right hand extended in that unanswerable gesture of fearlessness, bestowing on us the courage and confidence to follow that path to the end.

Amoghasiddhi is the Buddha of Action. The green Buddha does not sit on a calm ocean like Amitabha. Instead he is pulled through space by his bird-men, rushing onwards, to the stirring clash of their cymbals. His main emblem is the double vajra which must, in a sense, represent even greater harnessed energy than the single one, for it has an extra dimension. It is energy completely freed, capable of moving in any direction or in all directions at once.

It is for this reason that Amoghasiddhi is associated with the element air, and with sound, which moves out in all directions. In Tantric symbolism the air element is related to the throat chakra, which is concerned with communication. The quality of the sound produced when people speak is usually a very good indicator of their energy level.

The activity of Amoghasiddhi is spontaneous and altruistic. He moves out into the world as an expression of the compassionate heart of all the Buddhas. He and Amitabha form a complementary pair. Whereas Amitabha's compassionate influence is brought to bear on the world from the depths of meditation, Amoghasiddhi makes that influence tangible and visible. He could be said to represent *upaya*, the 'skilful means' by which Enlightened beings attract people to the Dharma. A Buddha will have a myriad ways of leading people away from samsara and on to the spiritual path. They will adopt any form, any mode of behaviour, necessary to put people in touch with the Dharma.

Another of Amoghasiddhi's connections is with volition – the will to act. It is volitions that create karma. We move towards some things and people, and away from (or against!) others. This constant mental movement produces consequences. As we saw when exploring Amitabha's realm, each of us creates a world in which to live, and it is through our volitions that we do this. If we are to 'stop the world' and get off the wheel of rebirth and suffering, our task is to prevent these volitions arising. As long as we are still emotionally entangled with the world, trying to force situations to continue or to disappear, our relationship with it will continue, and we shall not be free.

Amoghasiddhi's compassionate activity is spontaneous. He does not have to stop to work out the best course of action, or whom to help next. All his actions flow unpremeditated, arising naturally out of his panoramic awareness of situations.

It is this unpremeditated altruism which is born from the Wisdom of Amoghasiddhi, known as the All-Accomplishing Wisdom. The spiritual poison which he transmutes into this Wisdom is envy, that most barren and fruitless of feelings. We have seen how Amoghasiddhi's symbolism is concerned with the union of opposites. Fittingly, envy manages to unite craving with hatred or resentment. Envy wishes to succeed, but its eyes are on the external world and the accomplishments

of others. Amoghasiddhi teaches us to look within, to
mobilize our own resources. If we look deep enough, we
will see the illusory nature of self and other. Envy then
becomes equanimity.

Amoghasiddhi presides over the realm of the titans, or
asuras. These are represented in the Wheel of Life as
powerful, jealous beings, always in contention with the
gods. To employ stereotypes, they are the career politicians of our world, the young executives prepared to do
anything for a directorship. They are energetic and powerful. They despise weakness. The only things they re-
spect are power, energy, money, and success. It is no
good giving them sermons on gentleness and humility.
They will assume that you are someone weak trying to
trick them into giving up their superiority. Anyway, they
will probably not even stop to take in your arguments;
in the time they spend listening to you, one of their rivals
might get ahead of them.

To convert *asuras* to the Dharma, they need to see that
you have something that they do not. Only if you can
match their energy and resourcefulness will you get a
hearing. Angulimala listened to the Buddha only when
the Buddha had proved to have powers far beyond his
own.

For dealing with *asuras*, Amoghasiddhi has all the
power of the crossed vajras, all the energy of total action.
Asuras worship success, and his success is unobstructed
and infallible. Fearless, developed in a balanced way,
without a weakness for the *asuras* to exploit, he cannot
be defeated. He is someone to whom they are prepared

to listen, an ideal they can recognize. The dark green Buddha is a figure that even the jealous and suspicious heart of a titan can learn to love.

6

VAIROCHANA: THE ILLUMINATOR

AS WE SAW in Chapter 1, a mandala is not a flat, two-dimensional diagram. It is more like a many-storeyed golden mansion, or even a palace of crystal, in which a light in one room is reflected in all the others. In the last four sections we have entered the mandala and explored it by travelling in a circle. We could very profitably keep on circumambulating, meditating on each Buddha in turn, seeing new connections and taking the Buddhas more deeply into our consciousness. A mandala has many levels of meaning, and one cannot grasp them all at once. However, we shall only fully understand the mandala when we have come to its centre.

We have been well prepared to come to the heart of the mandala by the four Buddhas we have met. As we encountered them, each Buddha gave us a gift – something we needed to help prepare ourselves for a 'meeting' with ultimate Reality.

Akshobhya held up the crystal mirror of wisdom to show us the truth of things, to let us see ourselves as we are, undistorted. Then he tapped the earth, to remind us that we shall find truth not in our ideas about things but in direct experience.

However, the clear vision of Akshobhya could have been a little cold, a little hard. So Ratnasambhava gave us the jewel of beauty. He taught us to appreciate the beauty in nature, in the arts, in other people, in ourselves. He inspired us to mine within ourselves for the beauties of the Dharma, and to share them with others.

Then, lest we lose ourselves for ever in gazing into Ratnasambhava's jewel, Amitabha gave us a red lotus. He held out to us the soft, open flower of love and compassion, so that we began to open out to others, to soften our hearts, and to see the unique value of every living thing.

Finally, with a mere gesture of his right hand, Amoghasiddhi bestowed on us the gift of fearlessness, to venture into the world energetically helping all beings. More than that, he gave us the courage to enter the centre of the mandala, to gaze upon the centre of existence.

Light is, in reality, more awful than darkness. RUSKIN

At the heart of the mandala we find four great lions supporting a lotus throne on their backs. Above the lions, everything is white light: there is a white lotus, a white moon mat, and a white Buddha, smiling and serene, the colour of sunlight on snow, wearing ornate white robes. The only contrast is provided by his black hair, and a great golden wheel, a dharmachakra, which he clasps in his hands with a peculiar mudra. This is Vairochana, the Buddha whose name means 'Illuminator'. In the Nyingma system of practice which we are following here, it is he who sits in the heart of the mandala, the symbol and embodiment of absolute Reality. (In some forms of Tantric practice, Vairochana is in the east, with Akshobhya at the centre of the mandala.)

A dharmachakra or wheel of the Dharma

The Dharma wheel which Vairochana holds is the last gift of the Buddhas – the final thing we need. If we meditate on it long enough we shall arrive at Enlightenment.

This golden wheel is rich in symbolic meanings. In the Indian Buddhist mind, the golden wheel was associated with sovereignty. It is the emblem of the 'chakravartin raja' (wheel-turning king), a monarch who rules in accordance with the Dharma. Being a sincere Dharma practitioner himself, he uses the authority of his position to influence society in all kinds of positive ways. The descriptions of his attributes in Buddhist scriptures are important, as they serve as a reminder that Buddhism is concerned not just with individual development and retreat from the world. Buddhism aims to influence and transform society. This is worth doing in itself, but it also comes from the recognition that individual Dharma practice becomes extremely difficult if the culture and society in which you live are unsupportive of, or hostile to, your efforts.

The association of the wheel with kingship comes partly from an ancient Indian tradition, according to which the boundaries of a kingdom were established by setting loose a horse with a wheel on its back. Wherever it went unchallenged, the king's rule was accepted.

Another word for the Buddha's teaching is *sasana*. This means something like dispensation – the area over which an Enlightened mind holds sway. As the principles of the Dharma hold true throughout all universes, and there is nothing in time or space that can shake the mind of a Buddha, which encompasses it all, then in a sense the whole of time and space is the Buddha's domain, the sphere of influence of the Enlightened mind, of Vairochana.

At the time of his birth a sage prophesied that Siddhartha – the worldly name of the Buddha-to-be – would become either a great ruler or a Buddha. Despite his father's best efforts, Siddhartha came to see that ultimately even the greatest ruler has no control over anything; like Canute he is unable to hold back the waves of change, of sickness, and of death. A Buddha, on the other hand, in becoming master of his own consciousness, becomes possessed of the universe.

When, after his Enlightenment, the Buddha visited his family, his father reproached him for not wearing the robes befitting one of noble birth. The Buddha retorted that he came from the noblest lineage of all, that of the Enlightened, and that the rag robes he wore were the traditional garb of that noble lineage.

These paradoxes are made much of in the sutras. Though the Buddha is a beggar, he is more noble than the greatest king. Though he has nothing, his life is more pleasurable. Though he is unarmed, a king surrounded by his army is more frightened than he.

To give one small example, there is a canonical story (to be found in the Udana, a subdivision of the Pali Canon, which is a collection of discourses given by the Buddha Shakyamuni) of a monk called Bhaddiya, who used to be a king. His friends hear him sitting in the forest saying 'Ah, 'tis bliss, 'tis bliss!' They assume that he is recalling his days of pleasure and comfort as a king, and is dissatisfied with the spiritual life. They tell the Buddha this. He refuses to jump to conclusions, but asks Bhaddiya to come and see him, and questions him. Bhaddiya recounts how when he was a king he had a palace guarded inside and out, and still he felt his life was at risk. By comparison, the simple life of mental training in the forest is sheer bliss.

These stories counteract the idea people sometimes have that followers of the spiritual life are too weak and inadequate to succeed in the world. On the contrary, the Buddhist tradition shows that spiritual practitioners become kings among men and queens among women –

there are similar stories of female practitioners, and various queens have practised the Dharma. There is an important sutra in the Mahayana tradition (which comprises schools of Buddhism teaching the 'Great Way', that is to help all living beings escape from suffering) called *The Lion's Roar of Queen Shrimala*.

The spiritual life surpasses even the most elevated of worldly states, and it requires at least as much energy and courage to extend the empire of the Dharma as it does to extend a worldly kingdom. Not for nothing did the Buddha say that someone who had gained a spiritual victory over his lower nature had gained a greater victory than that involved in conquering a thousand men a thousand times in battle.

So the first message of the golden wheel is that by setting out on the spiritual path one joins the most noble of all lineages. Without preening ourselves or inflating our egos, if we are practitioners of the Dharma we should recognize that we need envy no one. The golden wheel also reminds us that we are practising so as to be able one day to affect all people. It helps us see that we cannot forget the world and society, but have to work positively within it, to create positive conditions for ourselves and others to practise the Dharma.

Vairochana means 'Illuminator', and it is clear that the golden wheel he holds in his hands is, symbolically, a great sun. The sun, of course, has legions of associations. For some races the sun is seen as a golden door to a higher dimension. In fact, just as all natural life depends upon it, the sun as symbol plays a major role in the

'psychic economy' of all human beings. For the vision-
ary or mystic it becomes far more than a ball of gas, and
represents the spiritual principle that illumines the
universe.

There are two attributes of the sun which make it a
particularly appropriate symbol for Buddhahood. The
first is the sun's centrality. It is the heart of the planets'
dance. Drawn to its light and warmth even cold Neptune
and Pluto follow it like lovers. You could look at the
mandala as a kind of planetary system, with four planets
– blue, yellow, red, and green – in orbit around Vairochana's golden wheel, and all deriving their light from
it. For, in a sense, the other four Buddhas are just partial
reflections of Vairochana.

His family is known simply as the Buddha or Tathagata family. (Tathagata, meaning 'thus gone', is another
epithet for someone who is fully Enlightened.) His Wisdom, the *dharmadhatu* (sphere of truth) Wisdom, is the
totality of all wisdom, embracing all those of the other
Buddhas. His white colour includes all colours, and the
other hues of the mandala are fragmentations of his pure
whiteness. It is his energy and intensity, his purity, that
we are seeing in other parts of the mandala, just as we
see the sun through the brilliant pieces of a great stained-
glass window.

The second attribute, complementary to the first, is the
sun's all-pervasiveness. The sun itself is like the hub of
the golden wheel, the spokes its rays, and the rim the
boundary of its vast sphere of influence. As the wheel is
a perfect circle, it suggests the absolute even-minded-

ness of the Enlightened Mind, its compassion shining equally on everything and everyone.

The golden wheel symbolizes the paradoxical nature of Vairochana. He sits at the centre of the mandala, at its hub, and yet the experience of total Enlightenment that he symbolizes is one of panoramic awareness without any central reference point. Vairochana is central to the whole mandala only in the sense that his Dharmadhatu Wisdom is the central experience of the spiritual life. In achieving this Wisdom we feel perfectly balanced, completely in harmony with everything. Yet, on attaining that Dharmadhatu Wisdom, we find that notions of centre and circumference disappear. There is no 'I' at the centre of the mandala to which everything is referred. At the centre of the mandala we find only panoramic awareness embracing the whole mandala. It is for this reason that Vairochana's Pure Land is called the All-Pervading Circle in Tibetan, and his element is space.

The Buddha's first teaching is traditionally referred to as his first 'turning, or setting in motion, of the wheel of the Dharma'. The mudra with which Vairochana holds the wheel is known as the mudra of turning the wheel of the Dharma. The golden wheel, then, symbolizes not only Buddhahood itself but also the Buddha's teaching, which leads to that Enlightened state. It is usually shown with eight spokes, which symbolize the Noble Eightfold Path. It is one of the commonest of all Buddhist symbols. The great Buddhist monastic university of Nalanda had as its crest this dharmachakra, supported on either side by deer – a reminder of the Deer Park at Sarnath where the Buddha first taught.

It seems likely that the figure of Vairochana appeared out of meditation on the Buddha Shakyamuni as teacher, which from our point of view is his most crucial function – if he had not bothered to teach there would be no Buddhism, and the path to Enlightenment would not be open to us. In the Mahayana sutras Shakyamuni is represented continuing to teach, turning the wheel of the Dharma eternally, seated on the Vulture's Peak – a site in northern India near the town of Rajagriha where the Buddha often stayed. In the Mahayana sutras it is transformed into the archetypal seat of teaching of the Buddha. Vairochana symbolizes this eternal teaching of the Dharma. He reminds us that within our own mind there always exists the possibility of total transformation.

In a sense we are confronting Vairochana's radiance all the time, although it is dimmed and diffused. However, this very phrase gives the game away. As long as 'we' are confronting 'it', we cannot be at the centre of the mandala. Our difficulty is that there is an 'I' which stands apart from Reality and experiences it as something outside ourselves. We remain cut off from it because we do not identify with all our experience. Often our identification is entirely with our body and its limited concerns. The rest of life we see as being separate from us. This, according to Buddhism, is the cause of all suffering.

How can we overcome this situation in which we are confronted by Reality but feel cut off from it? We can try to conquer the world and bring it under our sway – a strategy that can never work. Or we can give up all attempts at power and control and relate to the world through loving-kindness, in this way expanding our consciousness to include more and more people. We need to give up 'ego-imperialism', to stop being fixated on our own concerns. Then our mind begins to take on more of the expansive and all-pervading quality of Vairochana's wisdom. We come closer to Reality, closer to the centre of the mandala.

When we have seen through egotism and embraced loving-kindness towards all that lives we shall be ready to receive Vairochana's gift – the responsibility of sharing what we have learned with others. The final message of the mandala is that no experience is complete until it has been communicated. Keeping the truth to ourselves is a form of ego-imperialism.

We can say that it would not have been enough for Shakyamuni to spend the rest of his life sitting under the bodhi tree rapt with the bliss of Enlightenment. In a sense his experience of Enlightenment was only complete and fulfilling when he saw it mirrored in the understanding eyes of Kaundinya, the first disciple to deeply understand his teaching. Once we have entered and explored the mandala, it will not be enough to use its blueprint to make our own life a harmonious pattern. That is only the beginning. We have to enable all suffering sentient beings, all life, to come to the centre of the mandala.

One last association of the golden wheel points to how the mandala needs to keep expanding, how it is never finished, how it has within it the seeds of its own self-transcendence.

We have seen that the golden wheel is the sun of Reality, towards which we need to orient our lives. It is a symbol of the Buddha's spiritual kingship over the universe. It is also a symbol for the teaching, and the need to complete our experience of the spiritual path by sharing it with others. However, there is a further possible interpretation, which adds another dimension of meaning. This golden wheel that Vairochana holds could also be seen as the golden circle of the mandala itself.

Vairochana sits at the centre of the mandala, but paradoxically he is at the same time completely beyond it, holding it lightly in his hands, spinning it like a child's toy. Every step on the spiritual path, every step around the mandala, is an experience of self-transcendence. This is true not just of the path. Even the goal, Buddhahood itself, is a continuing process of evolution – moving to higher and higher levels in ways we cannot conceive. That is why at the centre of the mandala we meet a Buddha holding the mandala. At the centre of the mandala we transcend mandalas altogether.

CONCLUSION

WE HAVE NOW made the journey to the heart of the mandala and met all the Five Buddhas. However, reading our way around the mandala is only a beginning. We need to make the pilgrimage to meet the Five Buddhas repeatedly. In Tibetan Buddhist yogas this mandala is located in the heart centre of the meditator. What is at our heart centre is our core value, what we have set our heart upon, what moves and motivates us. This emphasizes that it is not enough to know about the Five Buddhas, one has to allow them to come alive in one's life.

How do we turn symbols from wooden pieces which we shuffle about on the board of our rational mind into living kings and queens in our heart's core? Firstly we have to dispense with, or at least put into suspension, limiting views which prevent us from being receptive to this transformation. Many of us have been taught to think of imagination and symbols as merely fantasy, having no power to change our lives. We have to open ourselves to the possibility that there are more things in heaven and earth and in the depths of our minds than are dreamt of in materialist philosophy. There is a work by Samuel Beckett called *Imagination Dead Imagine*. In contrast with the bleak universe depicted by Beckett, we need to envision what life would be like if our imagination came vividly to life, so that our whole sense of the world burst into flower. Then the Five Buddhas would not be symbols at all, but majestic presences filling our lives with light and wisdom.

Once you have taken off the blindfold of limiting views you then have to find ways of interacting with the Five Buddhas. There are traditional sadhanas – meditation practices – in which they are invoked. However, even if you are not performing these formal meditations, you can still find ways of opening yourself to these Buddhas' benign influence. You can circle the mandala in your mind's eye, seeing each Buddha in turn, with their colours, mudras, and distinctive symbols. You can paint them, or write poems weaving together some of their associations: their colour, time of day, direction, wisdom, and so forth. At times you may find yourself being especially drawn to one of the Buddhas, in which case you can particularly concentrate on that figure.

The most important thing is to enter into an emotional relationship with the Buddhas, so that calling one of them to mind or seeing a picture of them evokes a feeling of devotion, and brings with it a lightening of the load of mundane life. As this process continues, the Buddhas begin to fascinate, to gleam like jewels in the crown of the mind. Once the process reaches this stage, the wisdoms that the Buddhas embody will begin to shine through your mind, illuminating your life.

According to the Tibetan Buddhist tradition, embodied in the *bardo thödol* – popularly known in the West as the *Tibetan Book of the Dead* – if you have entered into a deep relationship with the Five Buddhas they will illuminate your death as well as your life. Unlike the materialist view, in which death is the point when the chemicals stop swilling round your brain causing the cancellation of your credit cards, Buddhism believes in a series of lives. For ordinary human beings this process of rebirth is one over which we have little or no control. As a result of producing mental states characterized by craving, aversion, and ignorance of the nature of our own minds, we are repeatedly reborn into forms of being in which we are subject to the sufferings of old age, sickness, and death. Through the practice of the Dharma we can bring this process of uncontrolled rebirth to an end.

For the Tibetan Buddhist tradition, death represents a great opportunity. For in this state of bardo – between one physical existence and the next – our consciousness is freed from the limitations of physical embodiment, and becomes very subtle, concentrated, and malleable. In this state of consciousness, given prior spiritual training, we have a real chance of recognizing the true nature of mind, and liberating ourselves for ever from uncontrolled rebirth. According to the *Tibetan Book of the Dead* these Five Buddhas will appear as visions during the bardo experience. If we have meditated on them whilst alive, then there is a good chance that in the bardo we shall meet them as old friends and recognize them as manifestations of our own minds. By doing so, we shall free ourselves from the whole round of unsatisfactory rebirths, and gain Enlightenment. Thus familiarizing our minds with these Five Buddhas can have profound implications for the whole future trend of our existence.

Whatever may come after death, by entering into relationship with the Five Buddhas here and now we can enrich our lives. For instance, by dwelling on Vairochana we can find a source of illumination within ourselves, an inner sun which can warm us and open our hearts in the midst of the worst storms of mundane life. By resting our minds on his figure holding the golden wheel of the Buddha's teaching, we can absorb the Dharma with our hearts just as much as if we were to read a Buddhist teaching. Each of the Five Buddhas has his own lessons of wisdom and compassion to impart to us. Together, however, they form an Enlightened network, which has yet more to teach us.

In the late eighties I visited a museum in Leiden in Holland. My companion, who knew the place well, led me through a whole series of rooms, including one full of dolls and puppets, until we came to a darkened room with a raised spotlit wooden platform. On this dais was a line of five wooden Buddhas, each several feet high, seated in silent meditation. Their features suggested that they were Chinese or Japanese. Three of them had their hands in the mudra of meditation, the other two were making a mudra which is associated in Far Eastern

Buddhism with Vairochana. Padded benches had been provided against the wall opposite the Buddhas, and a number of local people were sitting quietly, absorbing the atmosphere in the room. My friend and I joined them.

The figures were so well crafted, and the peacefulness in the room was so tangible, that after a while my mind began to respond to this line of seated figures as if I was in the presence of living Buddhas. Not only was each one impressively dignified and serene, they all seemed absorbed in a meditation which knew no beginning or end. What struck me most forcibly of all was an eerie sense that each of the five was in direct communication with each of the others, that they were all partaking in one meditation. Thus my mind on that winter's afternoon in Holland was catalysed by those five figures into an intuition of what Sangha – spiritual community – would be like at the highest level. The power of those five Buddhas together seemed much greater than five times one. They made me aware of the possibility of a mystical communion with others, in which the barriers separating us could come down completely.

Similarly our Five Buddhas, seated in perfect harmony within their mandala, are all in perfect communication. In fact one cannot define them either as five Buddhas or as one without leaving out part of the reality of the situation. Reflecting on this aspect of the mandala of the Five Buddhas can produce new and multiple understandings. In fact the potential for unfolding wisdom through contemplating this mandala is as limitless as the Enlightened mind itself.

CORRELATIONS	AKSHOBHYA	RATNASAMBHAVA
Meaning of name	The Immutable or Imperturbable	The Jewel-Born or Jewel-Producing
Colour	Deep blue	Yellow
Direction	East	South
Time of day	Dawn	Noon
Emblem	Vajra	Jewel
Family	Vajra	Ratna
Animal	Elephant	Horse
Mudra	Earth-touching (*bhumisparsha*)	Supreme Giving (*varada*)
Seed syllable	*hum*	*tram*
Mantra	*om vajra akshobhya hum*	*om ratnasambhava tram*
Wisdom	Mirror-Like	Sameness
Poison	Hatred	Pride
Element	Water	Earth
Pure Land	Abhirati (The Joyous)	Shrimat (The Glorious)
Realm	Hells	Human

AMITABHA	AMOGHASIDDHI	VAIROCHANA
Infinite Light	Unobstructed Success	The Illuminator
Red	Green	White
West	North	Centre
Sunset	Midnight	—
Lotus	Double vajra or sword	Golden *dharmachakra*
Padma	Karma kula	Buddha or Tathagata
Peacock	Garuda or bird-man	Lion
Meditation (*dhyana*)	Fearlessness (*abhaya*)	Turning the Wheel of the Dharma
hrih	*ah*	*om*
om amideva hrih	*om amoghasiddhi ah hum*	*om vairochana hum*
Discriminating	All-Accomplishing	Dharmadhatu
Greed	Envy	Ignorance
Fire	Air	Space
Sukhavati (The Happy Land)	Karmasampat (Perfected Good Actions)	Ghanavyuha (Densely Arrayed)
Hungry ghosts (*pretas*)	*Asuras* or titans	Gods

ILLUSTRATION CREDITS

INDEX

A

abhaya mudra 50, 75
Abhirati 17, 74
action 49, 54ff, 75,
    see also Buddha of Action
aesthetic appreciation 31ff
air 54, 75
Akshobhya 16ff, 40, 59, 60
All-Accomplishing Wisdom
    55, 75
All-Pervading Circle 65, 75
altruism 55
Amitabha 37ff, 54, 59
Amitayus 40
Amoghasiddhi 46ff, 59,
    see also Buddha of Action
anger 17
Angulimala 52, 56
archetypes 6
art 32

asuras 56, 75
Athena 18

B

Bach 31
bardo 71
bardo thödol 14, 71
beauty 31, 33, 59
Beckett, S. 70
Bhaddiya 62
bhumisparsha 22, 74
Blake, W. 32
Blücher, G.L. von 33
blue 74
Bodhicharyavatara 28
Bodhichitta 35
Buddha
    figure 41
    recollection of 5
    family 64, 75 *(contd.)*

Buddha *(contd.)*
  of Action 7, 54, *see also*
    Amoghasiddhi
  of Beauty 7, 31, *see also*
    Ratnasambhava
  of Giving 7, 26, *see also*
    Ratnasambhava
Buddhahood 68
Buddhism, Tibetan 14

C
Canute 61
chakra 54
chakravartin raja 60
chintamani 35
Chögyam Trungpa Rimpoche
  29
Christianity 41
co-operation 30
communication 54
Compassion 7, 37, 44, 59
confidence 16
cosmology 47
craving 40, *see also* greed
crucifix 41
culture 31
Cupid 13

D
Daito 43
death 53, 71
Devadatta 51
dharmachakra 65, 75,
  see also golden wheel

dharmadhatu 64
  Wisdom of 75
dhyana mudra 41, 43, 75
Discriminating Wisdom 38, 75
divine mansion 13
double vajra 46ff, 54, 75
dreams 6

E
earth 26, 74
Earth Goddess 22
earth-touching mudra 22, 74
Eightfold Path 65
elephant 16, 23, 51, 74
empathy 30
Emptiness 11, 44
energy 34, 46, 54
Enlightenment 7, 49, 67
envy 55, 75
equanimity 27

F
fear 53
fearlessness 50ff, 59
  mudra 75
fire 11, 39, 75
flames of shunyata 11

G
garuda 48, 75
giving 25, 28, 30, 36
  Buddha of 7, 26
  mudra of 28, 58, 74
Glorious, the 29, 74
gods 56, 75

golden wheel 60, 63, 65ff,
  see also dharmachakra
Govinda 48
greed 75, *see also* craving
Greek myths 18
green 75
Guhyaloka 1

H
hatred 19, 40, 74
horse 34, 74
human realm 30
hum 17
hungry ghost 40, 75
hybrid 49

I
ignorance 75
Illuminator 60, 63, 75
imagination 69
Imagination Dead Imagine 70
Imperturbable 74
individuation 8
Indra 18
Infinite Life 40
Infinite Light 37, 75
insecurity 30
insight 53
integration 9, 48ff
interpenetration 48

J
jewel 74
  family 28, 74
  -Born 26, 74

-Producing One 26, 74
  wish-fulfilling 35ff
Jina 15
Jung, C.G. 8

K
Kaundinya 67
kingship 61

L
Leiden 72
lion 59, 75
lotus 12, 19, 39, 59, 75
  family 39, 75
love 37, 44, 51, 59
loving-kindness 51, 67

M
Mahayana 17, 63
  sutras 66
maitri 51, *see also* love
makara 19
mandala 8ff, 58, 67,
  see also divine mansion
  features of 10ff
Mara 21ff
meditation 9, 41, 44
  mudra 41, 43, 75
Michelangelo 31
Midas 27
Middle Way 43
Mirror-Like Wisdom 24, 74
mudra
  earth-touching (*bhumisparsha*)
    22, 74 (*contd.*)

mudra (*contd.*)
  of fearlessness (*abhaya*) 50, 75
  of giving (*varada*), 28, 58, 74
  of meditation (*dhyana*) 41,
    43, 75
  of turning the wheel
    (*dharmachakrapravartana*)
    65, 75
myth 6

N

Nalanda 42, 65
Neptune 64
nirvana 19
Nyingma 14, 60

O

'Ozymandias' 26

P

Pali Canon 62
passion 38
peacock 39, 75
Pegasus 35
Perfection of Wisdom in 8,000 Lines 18
playfulness 34
Pluto 64
pride 26, 30, 34, 74
Pure Land
  of Akshobhya (Abhirati) 17,
    24, 74
  of Amitabha (Sukhavati) 44,
    75
  of Amoghasiddhi
    (Karmasampat) 75
  of Ratnasambhava
    (Shrimat) 29, 74
  of Vairochana
    (Ghanavyuha) 65, 75

R

raga 38
Rajagriha 66
Raphael 31
Ratna family 28
Ratnasambhava 25ff, 38, 59
realms 26
rebirth 71
recollection of the Buddha 5
red 37, 75

S

samsara 19
samurai 43
Sarnath 66
sasana 61
Shakespeare, W. 31
Shakyamuni 5, 17, 21ff, 49, 50,
  62, 66, 67
shang-shang 48
Shantideva 28
Shelley, P.B. 26
shunyata 11
Siddhartha 61
six realms 26
skilful means 54
Sona 43

space 65, 75
suffering 66
Sukhavati 75
sun 63
sunset 38
symbols 3, 69

T
Tantra 10, 14, 20
Tathagata family 64, 75
teacher 66
Thor 18
throat chakra 54
thunderbolt 18
Tibetan Book of the Dead 14, 71
titans 56, 75
transformation 11

U
Udana 62
universe 47
Unobstructed Success 46, 75
upaya 54
Uriah Heep 30
utilitarianism 33
Uttarakuru 75

V
Vairochana 60ff

vajra 11f, 18ff, 74
   family 18, 40, 74
   double 46ff, 54, 75
vajrasana 21
varada mudra 28, 58, 74
victory 63
Vishalaksha 17
volition 55
Vulture's Peak 66

W
water 23, 74
wealth 28ff
Wheel of Life 26
wheel-turning king 60
white 59, 64, 75
windhorse 35
Wisdom 7, 11, 24, 59, 74
   of Equality or Sameness
      26ff, 32, 38, 74
   of the dharmadhatu 64
wish-fulfilling jewel 35ff
Wordsworth, W. 33

Y
yellow 74

Z
Zeus 18

The Windhorse symbolizes the energy of the enlightened mind carrying the Three Jewels – the Buddha, the Dharma, and the Sangha – to all sentient beings.

Buddhism is one of the fastest-growing spiritual traditions in the Western world. Throughout its 2,500-year history, it has always succeeded in adapting its mode of expression to suit whatever culture it has encountered.

Windhorse Publications aims to continue this tradition as Buddhism comes to the West. Today's Westerners are heirs to the entire Buddhist tradition, free to draw instruction and inspiration from all the many schools and branches. Windhorse publishes works by authors who not only understand the Buddhist tradition but are also familiar with Western culture and the Western mind.

For orders and catalogues contact

WINDHORSE PUBLICATIONS	WINDHORSE BOOKS	WEATHERHILL INC
11 PARK ROAD	P O BOX 574	41 MONROE TURNPIKE
BIRMINGHAM	NEWTON	TRUMBULL
B13 8AB	NSW 2042	CT 06611
UK	AUSTRALIA	USA

Windhorse Publications is an arm of the Friends of the Western Buddhist Order, which has more than sixty centres on five continents. Through these centres, members of the Western Buddhist Order offer regular programmes of events for the general public and for more experienced students. These include meditation classes, public talks, study on Buddhist themes and texts, and 'bodywork' classes such as t'ai chi, yoga, and massage. The FWBO also runs several retreat centres and the Karuna Trust, a fund-raising charity that supports social welfare projects in the slums and villages of India.

Many FWBO centres have residential spiritual communities and ethical businesses associated with them. Arts activities are encouraged too, as is the development of strong bonds of friendship between people who share the same ideals. In this way the FWBO is developing a unique approach to Buddhism, not simply as a set of techniques, less still as an exotic cultural interest, but as a creatively directed way of life for people living in the modern world.

If you would like more information about the FWBO please write to

LONDON BUDDHIST CENTRE	ARYALOKA
51 ROMAN ROAD	HEARTWOOD CIRCLE
LONDON	NEWMARKET
E2 0HU	NH 03857
UK	USA

ALSO FROM WINDHORSE

VESSANTARA

MEETING THE BUDDHAS: A GUIDE TO BUDDHAS, BODHISATTVAS, AND TANTRIC DEITIES

Sitting poised and serene upon fragrant lotus blooms, they offer smiles of infinite tenderness, immeasurable wisdom. Bellowing formidable roars of angry triumph from the heart of blazing infernos, they dance on the naked corpses of their enemies.

Who are these beings – the Buddhas, Bodhisattvas, and Protectors, the 'angry demons' and 'benign deities' – of the Buddhist Tantric tradition? Are they products of an alien, even disturbed, imagination? Or are they, perhaps, real? What have they got to do with Buddhism? And what have they got to do with us?

In this vivid informed account, an experienced Western Buddhist guides us into the heart of this magical realm and introduces us to the miraculous beings who dwell there.

368 pages, with text illustrations and colour plates
ISBN 0 904766 53 5
£14.99/$29.95

SANGHARAKSHITA

TIBETAN BUDDHISM: AN INTRODUCTION

A glorious past, a traumatic present, an uncertain future. What are we to make of Tibetan Buddhism?

Sangharakshita has spent many years in contact with Tibetan lamas of all schools, within the context of a wide experience of the Buddhist tradition as a whole. He is admirably qualified as a guide through the labyrinth that is Tibetan Buddhism. In this book he gives a down-to-earth account of the origin and history of Buddhism in Tibet, and explains the essentials of this practical tradition which has much to teach us.

As the essence of Tibetan Buddhism is revealed, it is shown to be a beautiful and noble tradition which – and this is the important thing – can help us contact a sense of beauty and nobility in our lives.

144 pages, illustrated
ISBN 0 904766 86 1
£7.99/$15.95

SANGHARAKSHITA

RITUAL AND DEVOTION IN BUDDHISM:
AN INTRODUCTION

For many people in the West, devotional practice is a confronting aspect of
Buddhism which it is easier to ignore. Skilfully steering us through the
difficulties we may encounter, Sangharakshita shows that ritual and devotion
have a crucial role to play in our spiritual lives, because they speak the
language of the heart. Leading us through the Sevenfold Puja, a poetic
sequence of devotional moods, he gives us a feeling for the depth of spiritual
practice to be contacted through recitation, making offerings, and chanting
mantras.

  Knowledge alone cannot take us far along the spiritual path. This book
reveals the power of devotional practices to help us commit ourselves to
spiritual change with all our hearts.

128 pages
ISBN 0 904766 87 X
£6.99/$13.95

SIR EDWIN ARNOLD

THE LIGHT OF ASIA

This inspiring poem by Sir Edwin Arnold (1832–1904), though written more
than a hundred years ago, retains the power to move us in a way that no
prose rendering of the life of the Buddha can. We cannot but admire the
courage, determination, and self-sacrifice of the Indian prince who, out of
compassion, left his palace to find a remedy for the sufferings of the world.

192 pages, hardback, with glossary
ISBN 1 899579 19 2
£ 9.99/$19.95

TEJANANDA

THE BUDDHIST PATH TO AWAKENING

The word *Buddha* means 'one who is awake'. In this accessible introduction, Tejananda alerts us to the Buddha's wake-up call, illustrating how the Buddhist path can help us develop a clearer mind and a more compassionate heart.

Drawing on over twenty years experience of Buddhist meditation and study, Tejananda gives us a straightforward and encouraging description of the path of the Buddha and his followers – the path that leads ultimately to our own 'awakening'.

224 pages, with diagrams
ISBN 1 899579 02 8
£8.99/$17.95

KAMALASHILA

MEDITATION: THE BUDDHIST WAY OF TRANQUILLITY AND INSIGHT

A comprehensive guide to the methods and theory of Buddhist meditation, written in an informal, accessible style. It provides a complete introduction to the basic techniques, as well as detailed advice for more experienced meditators seeking to deepen their practice.

The author is a long-standing member of the Western Buddhist Order, and has been teaching meditation since 1975. In 1979 he helped to establish a semi-monastic community in North Wales, which has now grown into a public retreat centre. For more than a decade he and his colleagues developed approaches to meditation that are firmly grounded in Buddhist tradition but readily accessible to people with a modern Western background. Their experience – as meditators, as students of the traditional texts, and as teachers – is distilled in this book.

304 pages, with charts and illustrations
ISBN 1 899579 05 2
£12.99/$25.95